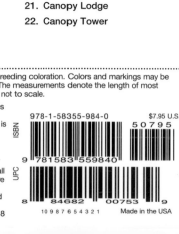

Mixed evergreen and deciduous forest

Swamp and seasonally flooded areas

Evergreen forest

Highland evergreen forest

Scrub, savannah, and crops

One of the premier birding destinations on earth, Panama has over 1,000 species of which 107 are regional endemics. Pipeline road has set the world record for 24-hour bird counts several times, tallying nearly 400 species in a single day. The country features a diverse array of habitats to support the vast number of species including some of the most accessible rainforests in the world.

Most illustrations show the adult male in breeding coloration. Colors and markings may be duller or absent during different seasons. The measurements denote the length of most species from bill to tail tip. Illustrations are not to scale.

Waterford Press produces reference guides that introduce novices to nature, science, travel and languages. Product information is featured on the website:
www.waterfordpress.com

Text and illustrations © 2020 by Waterford Press Inc. All rights reserved. Cover images © Shutterstock. To order, call 800-434-2555. For permissions, or to share comments, e-mail editor@waterfordpress.com. For information on custom-published products, call 800-434-2555 or e-mail info@waterfordpress.com. 200918

A POCKET NATURALIST® GUIDE

PANAMA BIRDS

A Folding Pocket Guide to Familiar Species

T0123947

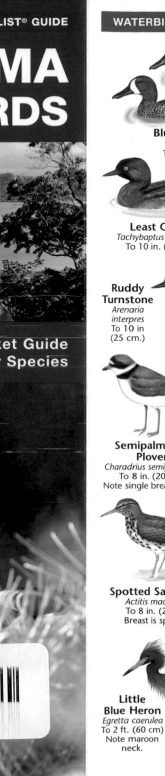

Blue-winged Teal
Anas discors
To 16 in. (40 cm)

Black-bellied Whistling-Duck
Dendrocygna autumnalis
To 21 in. (53 cm)

Least Grebe
Tachybaptus dominicus
To 10 in. (25 cm)

Winter

Sanderling
Calidris alba
To 8 in. (20 cm)
Runs in and out with waves along shorelines.

Whimbrel
Numenius phaeopus
To 20 in. (50 cm)
Note striped crown.

Ruddy Turnstone
Arenaria interpres
To 10 in. (25 cm.)

Semipalmated Plover
Charadrius semipalmatus
To 8 in. (20 cm)
Note single breast band.

Willet
Tringa semipalmata
To 17 in. (43 cm)
Wings flash black-and-white in flight.

American Oystercatcher
Haematopus palliatus
To 20 in. (50 cm)
Note red bill and black head.

Spotted Sandpiper
Actitis macularius
To 8 in. (20 cm)
Breast is spotted.

Killdeer
Charadrius vociferus
To 12 in. (30 cm)
Note two breast bands.

Southern Lapwing
Vanellus chilensis
To 12 in. (30 cm)

Little Blue Heron
Egretta caerulea
To 2 ft. (60 cm)
Note maroon neck.

Black-necked Stilt
Himantopus mexicanus
To 17 in. (43 cm)

White Ibis
Eudocimus albus
To 28 in. (70 cm)
The similar glossy ibis has red-brown plumage.

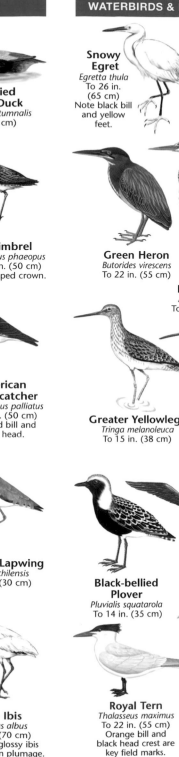

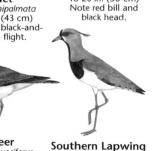

Snowy Egret
Egretta thula
To 26 in. (65 cm)
Note black bill and yellow feet.

Great Egret
Ardea alba
To 38 in. (95 cm)
Note yellow bill and black feet.

Yellow-crowned Night-Heron
Nyctanassa violacea
To 28 in. (70 cm)

Green Heron
Butorides virescens
To 22 in. (55 cm)

Great Blue Heron
Ardea herodias
To 4.5 ft. (1.4 m)

Cattle Egret
Bubulcus ibis
To 20 in. (50 cm)

Rufescent Tiger-Heron
Tigrisoma lineatum
To 28 in. (70 cm)

Greater Yellowlegs
Tringa melanoleuca
To 15 in. (38 cm)

Wilson's Snipe
Gallinago delicata
To 12 in. (30 cm)

Roseate Spoonbill
Platalea ajaja
To 32 in. (80 cm)
Bill is flattened at the tip.

Black-bellied Plover
Pluvialis squatarola
To 14 in. (35 cm)

Magnificent Frigatebird
Fregata magnificens
To 40 in. (1 m)
Note red throat, long wingspan and forked tail. Females have a white breast.

Tricolored Heron
Egretta tricolor
To 26 in. (65 cm)
Note white belly.

Royal Tern
Thalasseus maximus
To 22 in. (55 cm)
Orange bill and black head crest are key field marks.

Wattled Jacana
Jacana jacana
To 9 in. (23 cm)

Laughing Gull
Leucophaeus atricilla
To 18 in. (45 cm)

Anhinga
Anhinga anhinga
To 3 ft. (90 cm)

Common Gallinule
Gallinula galeata
To 14 in. (35 cm)

Neotropic Cormorant
Phalacrocorax brasilianus
To 26 in. (65 cm)
Often perches with wings open to help them dry out.

Purple Gallinule
Porphyrio martinicus
To 13 in. (33 cm)

Brown Pelican
Pelecanus occidentalis
To 50 in. (1.3 m)

American Coot
Fulica americana
To 16 in. (40 cm)
Note stout white bill.

HUMMINGBIRDS

Rufous-tailed Hummingbird
Amazilia tzacatl
To 4 in. (10 cm)

Purple-throated Mountain-gem
Lampornis calolaema
To 4 in. (10 cm)

Purple-crowned Fairy
Heliothryx barroti
To 4.5 in. (11 cm)

Long-billed Hermit
Phaethornis longirostris
To 6 in. (15 cm)

Violet Sabrewing
Campylopterus hemileucurus
To 6 in. (15 cm)

Snow-bellied Hummingbird
Amazilia edward
To 4 in. (10 cm)

Stripe-throated Hermit
Phaethornis striigularis
To 4 in. (10 cm)

Violet-crowned Woodnymph
Thalurania colombica
To 4 in. (10 cm)

White-necked Jacobin
Florisuga mellivora
To 4.5 in. (11 cm)

Black-throated Mango
Anthracothorax nigricollis
To 4.5 in. (12 cm)

White-vented Plumeleteer
Chalybura buffonii
To 4.5 in. (12 cm)

Violet-bellied Hummingbird
Damophila julie
To 3.5 in. (9 cm)

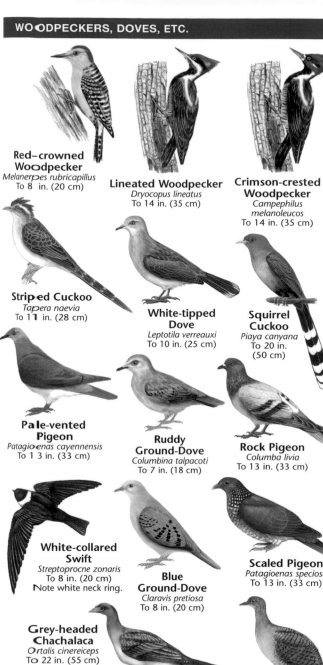

Red-crowned Woodpecker
Melanerpes rubricapillus
To 8 in. (20 cm)

Lineated Woodpecker
Dryocopus lineatus
To 14 in. (35 cm)

Crimson-crested Woodpecker
Campephilus melanoleucos
To 14 in. (35 cm)

Striped Cuckoo
Tapera naevia
To 11 in. (28 cm)

White-tipped Dove
Leptotila verreauxi
To 10 in. (25 cm)

Squirrel Cuckoo
Piaya cayana
To 20 in. (50 cm)

Pale-vented Pigeon
Patagioenas cayennensis
To 13 in. (33 cm)

Ruddy Ground-Dove
Columbina talpacoti
To 7 in. (18 cm)

Rock Pigeon
Columba livia
To 13 in. (33 cm)

White-collared Swift
Streptoprocne zonaris
To 8 in. (20 cm)
Note white neck ring.

Blue Ground-Dove
Claravis pretiosa
To 8 in. (20 cm)

Scaled Pigeon
Patagioenas speciosa
To 13 in. (33 cm)

Grey-headed Chachalaca
Ortalis cinereiceps
To 22 in. (55 cm)

Crested Guan
Penelope purpurascens
To 3 ft. (90 cm)

Great Tinamou
Tinamus major
To 18 in. (45 cm)
One of four similar species.

TROGONS, PARROTS, ETC.

Black-throated Trogon
Trogon rufus
To 9 in. (23 cm)

Slaty-tailed Trogon
Trogon massena
To 12 in. (30 cm)

Violaceous Trogon
Trogon violaceus
To 9 in. (23 cm)

Resplendent Quetzal
Pharomachrus mocinno
To 15 in. (38 cm)

Brown-hooded Parrot
Pyrilia haematotis
To 9 in. (23 cm)

Red-lored Parrot
Amazona autumnalis
To 13 in. (33 cm)

Mealy Parrot
Amazona farinosa
To 16 in. (40 cm)
Note bluish crown.

White-crowned Parrot
Pionus senilis
To 10 in. (25 cm)

Yellow-crowned Parrot
Amazona ochrocephala
To 12 in. (30 cm)

Brown-throated Parakeet
Aratinga pertinax
To 9 in. (23 cm)

Orange-chinned Parakeet
Brotogeris jugularis
To 7 in. (18 cm)

Crimson-fronted Parrot
Aratinga finschi
To 10 in. (25 cm)

Blue-and-Yellow Macaw
Ara ararauna
To 34 in. (85 cm)

Scarlet Macaw
Ara macao
To 34 in. (85 cm)

Red-and-Green Macaw
Ara chloropterus
To 38 in. (95 cm)

Blue-headed Parrot
Pionus menstruus
To 11 in. (28 cm)

TOUCANS, KINGFISHERS, ETC.

Collared Aracari
Pteroglossus torquatus
To 16 in. (40 cm)

Fiery-billed Aracari
Pteroglossus frantzii
To 17 in. (43 cm)

Great Jacamar
Jacamerops aureus
To 11 in. (28 cm)

Chestnut-mandibled Toucan
Ramphastos swainsonii
To 22 in. (55 cm)

Keel-billed Toucan
Ramphastos sulfuratus
To 19 in. (48 cm)

White-necked Puffbird
Notharchus hyperrhynchus
To 10 in. (25 cm)

Blue-throated Toucanet
Aulacorhynchus caeruleogularis
To 12 in. (30 cm)

Green Kingfisher
Chloroceryle americana
To 8 in. (20 cm)
The similar Amazon kingfisher is larger
(12 in./30 cm).

Ringed Kingfisher
Megaceryle torquata
To 14 in. (35 cm)

Smooth-billed Ani
Crotophaga ani
To 12 in. (30 cm)

Blue-crowned Motmot
Momotus momota
To 17 in. (43 cm)

Rufous Motmot
Baryphthengus martii
To 18 in. (45 cm)
Note 'racquet-tipped' tail feathers.

OWLS

Spectacled Owl
Pulsatrix perspicillata
To 18 in. (45 cm)

Mottled Owl
Ciccaba virgata
To 12 in. (30 cm)

Barn Owl
Tyto alba
To 20 in. (50 cm)
Note heart-shaped face.

BIRDS OF PREY

Turkey Vulture
Cathartes aura
To 32 in. (80 cm)
Note two-toned under-wings and red head.

King Vulture
Sarcoramphus papa
To 32 in. (80 cm)

Black Vulture
Coragyps atratus
To 27 in. (68 cm)

Harpy Eagle
Harpia harpyja
To 40 in. (1 m)
The largest raptor in the Americas. Panama's national bird.

White Hawk
Leucopternis albicollis
To 23 in. (58 cm)

Roadside Hawk
Buteo magnirostris
To 16 in. (40 cm)
Note rufous barring on chest.

Crested Caracara
Caracara cheriway
To 25 in. (63 cm)
Note red face and black head crest.

American Kestrel
Falco sparverius
To 12 in. (30 cm)

Gray Hawk
Buteo nitidus
To 17 in. (43 cm)
Note dark barring on chest.

Yellow-headed Caracara
Milvago chimachima
To 18 in. (45 cm)

Swallow-tailed Kite
Elanoides forficatus
To 2 ft. (60 cm)

Osprey
Pandion haliaetus
To 2 ft. (60 cm)

Laughing Falcon
Herpetotheres cachinnans
To 22 in. (55 cm)
Named for its cackling, laughing call.

Ornate Hawk-Eagle
Spizaetus ornatus
To 27 in. (68 cm)

Great Black Hawk
Buteogallus urubitinga
To 26 in. (65 cm)

PERCHING BIRDS

Barred Antshrike
Thamnophilus doliatus
To 6 in. (15 cm)

Western Slaty-Antshrike
Thamnophilus atrinucha
To 6 in. (15 cm)

Woodcreeper
Xiphorhynchus/ Dendrocolaptes/ Lepidocolaptes spp.
To 9 in. (23 cm)
Several similar species feed by probing for insects on tree trunks.

Tropical Kingbird
Tyrannus melancholicus
To 8 in. (20 cm)

Social Flycatcher
Myiozetetes similis
To 6 in. (15 cm)

Great Kiskadee
Pitangus sulphuratus
To 9 in. (23 cm)

Common Tody-Flycatcher
Todirostrum cinereum
To 9 in. (23 cm)

Fork-tailed Flycatcher
Tyrannus savana
To 16 in. (40 cm)

Boat-billed Flycatcher
Megarhynchus pitangua
To 9 in. (23 cm)

Collared Redstart
Myioborus torquatus
To 5 in. (13 cm)

Dot-winged Antwren
Microrhopias quixensis
To 4 in. (10 cm)

Blue Cotinga
Cotinga nattererii
To 8 in. (20 cm)

Southern Rough-winged Swallow
Stelgidopteryx ruficollis
To 5 in. (13 cm)

Barn Swallow
Hirundo rustica
To 8 in. (20 cm)
Note deeply forked tail.

Gray-breasted Martin
Progne chalybea
To 7 in. (18 cm)

PERCHING BIRDS

Variable Seedeater
Sporophila corvina
To 4 in. (10 cm)

Ruddy-breasted Seedeater
Sporophila minuta
To 4 in. (10 cm)

Clay-colored Thrush
Turdus greyi
To 10 in. (25 cm)

Bronzed Cowbird
Molothrus aeneus
To 9 in. (23 cm)

Blue Dacnis
Dacnis cayana
To 5 in. (13 cm)

Eastern Meadowlark
Sturnella magna
To 9 in. (23 cm)

Red-capped Manakin
Ceratopipra mentalis
To 4 in. (10 cm)

Great-tailed Grackle
Quiscalus mexicanus
To 18 in. (45 cm)
Long tail is keel-shaped.

Red-breasted Blackbird
Leistes militaris
To 7.5 in. (19 cm)

Blue-crowned Manakin
Lepidothrix coronata
To 3 in. (8 cm)

Black-chested Jay
Cyanocorax affinis
To 13.5 in. (34 cm)

Bananaquit
Coereba flaveola
To 5 in. (13 cm)

Yellow-faced Grassquit
Tiaris olivaceus
To 3.5 in. (9 cm)

Blue-black Grassquit
Volatinia jacarina
To 4 in. (10 cm)

Yellow-rumped Cacique
Cacicus cela
To 12 in. (30 cm)

PERCHING BIRDS

Palm Tanager
Thraupis palmarum
To 8 in. (20 cm)

Blue-grey Tanager
Thraupis episcopus
To 6 in. (15 cm)

Golden-hooded Tanager
Tangara larvata
To 5 in. (13 cm)

Plain-colored Tanager
Tangara inornata
To 5 in. (13 cm)

Crimson-backed Tanager
Ramphocelus dimidiatus
To 7 in. (18 cm)

Flame-colored Tanager
Piranga bidentata
To 7 in. (18 cm)

Summer Tanager
Piranga rubra
To 8 in. (20 cm)

Yellow-backed Oriole
Icterus chrysater
To 8 in. (20 cm)

Rufous-capped Warbler
Basileuterus rufifrons
To 5 in. (13 cm)

Thick-billed Euphonia
Euphonia laniirostris
To 4 in. (10 cm)

Buff-throated Saltator
Saltator maximus
To 8 in. (20 cm)

Red-legged Honeycreeper
Cyanerpes cyaneus
To 5 in. (13 cm)

Chestnut-headed Oropendola
Psarocolius wagleri
To 14 in. (35 cm)

Masked Tityra
Tityra semifasciata
To 8 in. (20 cm)

Lesser Goldfinch
Spinus psaltria
To 4.5 in. (11 cm)